WHALES SET II

BAIRD'S BEAKED WHALES

Kristin Petrie
ABDO Publishing Company

visit us at
www.abdopub.com

Published by ABDO Publishing Company, 4940 Viking Drive, Edina, Minnesota 55435.
Copyright © 2006 by Abdo Consulting Group, Inc. International copyrights reserved in all
countries. No part of this book may be reproduced in any form without written permission from
the publisher. The Checkerboard Library™ is a trademark and logo of ABDO Publishing
Company.

Printed in the United States.

Cover Photo: © Todd Pusser / SeaPics.com
Interior Photos: Corbis p. 4; Corel pp. 13, 17, 19; © Peggy Stapp / SeaPics.com pp. 15, 18;
   © Todd Pusser / SeaPics.com pp. 5, 8, 11, 21; Uko Gorter pp. 6-7

Series Coordinator: Stephanie Hedlund
Editors: Megan M. Gunderson, Stephanie Hedlund
Art Direction & Maps: Neil Klinepier

Library of Congress Cataloging-in-Publication Data

Petrie, Kristin, 1970-
   Baird's beaked whales / Kristin Petrie.
      p. cm. -- (Whales. Set II)
   Includes index.
   ISBN 1-59679-306-6
   1. Baird's beaked whale--Juvenile literature. I. Title.

QL737.C438P48 2005
599.5'45--dc22

                                                            2005043275

CONTENTS

Baird's Beaked Whales and Family

Whales are mammals. Monkeys, cats, dogs, and humans are, too. All mammals have hair, give birth to

live young, and feed their young milk. But most whales lose their hair after birth.

There are about 120 families of whales. One family is the Ziphiidae, or beaked whales. As you may have guessed, these whales have a long snout called a beak. This feature makes them look a bit like a dolphin.

The Baird's beaked whale is named after Spencer F. Baird. Baird was a naturalist and the secretary of the Smithsonian Institution.

There are different varieties of beaked whales. The largest is the *Berardius bairdii*, or Baird's beaked whale. These whales stick to the deepest parts of the ocean and stay clear of ships. So, we do not know how many there are. But, we do know they are not **endangered**.

Baird's beaked whales sometimes breach, or jump out of the water and splash back down. But, they spend most of their time deep underwater.

SHAPE, SIZE, AND COLOR

The Baird's beaked whale has a rounded body. It tapers at both ends to a slim head and tail. The head is small, but it features a bulging forehead and a long snout. A single blowhole can be found behind this bulge.

Like all whales, Baird's beaked whales have a tail and flippers. Their tail moves up and down to help them swim. Their flippers keep the whales balanced and help them steer.

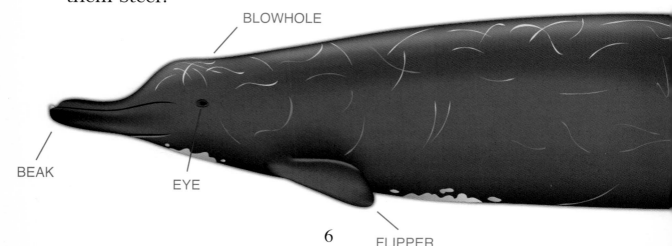

BLOWHOLE

BEAK

EYE

6

FLIPPER

The Baird's beaked whale's flippers fit into slight notches on its sides. This makes the whale more **streamlined**, so it can swim faster.

Baird's beaked whales are a medium-sized, toothed whale. Their average weight is 11 tons (10 t)! The average length of a male is 39 feet (12 m). Females can grow to more than 42 feet (13 m) long.

Some Baird's beaked whales are bluish gray, while others are almost black. They all have patches of lighter colors on their bellies. Many beaked whales have scars and scratches on their backs and sides. These are usually from other beaked whales or from **predators**.

DORSAL FIN

A Baird's Beaked Whale

TAIL

WHERE THEY LIVE

To avoid **predators**, beaked whales stay away from land. They prefer the deep, distant parts of the ocean. In fact, Baird's beaked whales are most often found at depths of about 3,300 feet (1,000 m).

Baird's beaked whales live in the North Pacific Ocean. They like **temperate** waters. For this reason, Baird's beaked whales **migrate** with the seasons.

In the summer months, the whales head north. The water is more to their liking in the Bering Sea around Alaska and Russia. They

Baird's beaked whales migrate in small pods. They are often seen in groups of three.

can also be found along the **continental slope** near California and Japan.

In the winter, Baird's beaked whales are rarely seen. So, their location is not known. But, many believe that they do not go farther south than Baja California.

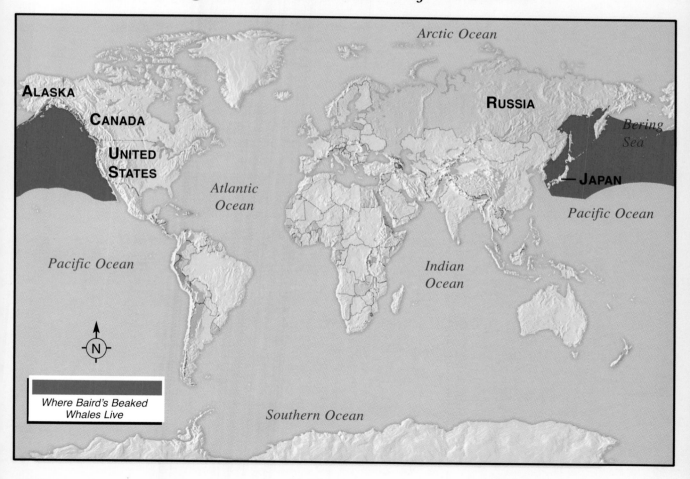

ALASKA

CANADA

UNITED STATES

RUSSIA

Bering Sea

JAPAN

Arctic Ocean

Atlantic Ocean

Pacific Ocean

Pacific Ocean

Indian Ocean

N

Where Baird's Beaked Whales Live

Southern Ocean

SENSES

The North Pacific Ocean is a big area for these whales to cover. To see where they are going, whales have eyes on the sides of their heads. These eyes are adapted to seeing underwater. However, beaked whales also use sounds to guide them.

Whales also have ears, but you can't see them. That is because they are hidden in the whale's **blubber**. Still, all **cetaceans** use sounds to communicate. Some mammals also use echolocation to "see" what is around them. Baird's beaked whales are some of those mammals.

With echolocation, the sound a mammal makes travels through the water. Then it hits an object and bounces off. When the noise returns, the mammal uses it to create a picture in its mind. Now it can find its friends, locate food, or hide from a **predator**!

Baird's beaked whales use clicks and moaning sounds to communicate with each other. Sound travels well in water. So, some whales may be heard from miles away.

Even though beaked whales have long snouts, they have little or no sense of smell. However, whales may have another sense. Researchers believe marine animals can detect changes in Earth's **magnetic field**. This helps them determine where they are.

DEFENSE

Whales use all of their senses to locate **predators**. Because Baird's beaked whales are so large, they have few natural enemies. But, cookie-cutter sharks and killer whales like to eat them.

Baird's beaked whales are difficult to catch for any predator. These whales dive to extreme depths when they sense danger. In other words, they hide!

Baird's beaked whales use another defense to avoid predators. A large group of whales is more difficult for a predator to attack. So, these whales bunch together and swim faster when they are frightened. These actions keep the whales safe.

Humans are the Baird's beaked whale's main threat. Russian, Canadian, Japanese, and U.S. whaling companies have hunted them in the past. In 1952, whaling cannons were used to catch more than 300 of these whales. Today, only 62 of them may be caught each year.

When Baird's beaked whales are being chased, they move as one unit. Jumping, diving, and changing direction occurs at the same time for the entire pod.

FOOD

Baird's beaked whales only have a couple natural **predators**. But, they eat many other animals. Their favorite meals are squid, octopuses, mackerel, sardines, and other deep-sea fish.

Some whales just swim with their mouths open to capture prey. They are **baleen** whales. But, Baird's beaked whales are toothed whales. These whales chase and catch their prey.

Baird's beaked whales have four teeth in the lower jaw. This is the only beaked whale species that has that many teeth. The lower jaw sticks out, so the teeth are visible even when the whale's mouth is closed.

The teeth of a Baird's beaked whale are used to grab and hold food. The whale then eats the food whole, like other whales. A Baird's beaked whale can have up to nine compartments in its stomach. So, it does not need to chew food to **digest** it.

The Baird's beaked whale uses its teeth to grab prey, but not to chew it.

BABIES

Baird's beaked whales eat a lot of food so they have energy to **migrate** and reproduce. They are ready to mate when they are 32 to 35 feet (10 to 11 m) long. Mating frequently takes place in the summer.

The female whale is called a cow. A Baird's beaked cow gives birth to a single whale about every three years. It carries the live baby for 10 to 17 months! This is the longest **pregnancy** of any **cetacean**.

The baby whale is called a calf. At birth, the calf is already 15 feet (5 m) long. Like other mammals, a cow nurses her calf with milk. This takes place until the calf can feed itself. Baird's beaked calves can nurse for two years or longer.

A Baird's beaked whale is fully grown when it is 15 years old. On average, they live for 70 years. Some of them live longer. The oldest Baird's beaked whale recorded was 84.

Male Baird's beaked whales are important to the pod. Some scientists believe elder males help the older calves. This may allow females to give birth more often.

BEHAVIORS

Baird's beaked whales stay in close-knit groups. These groups are called pods. A Baird's beaked pod can have anywhere from 3 to 30 members. But, it usually only has three to six individuals.

The blow of a Baird's beaked whale is much like many other cetaceans.

Pods move together when they are feeding and diving. Baird's beaked whales can stay at great depths for up to an hour. When they are not threatened, their dives are shorter. Then, pods surface every 20 to 30 minutes.

Like all whales, Baird's beaked whales exhale when they reach the surface. This produces a **blow**. Scientists often use the blow to identify a whale species.

18

However, the Baird's beaked whale does not have a special **blow**. So, this does not help with identification.

Whales often play with the members of their pod. They may breach or **spyhop**. These behaviors make Baird's beaked whales a magnificent sight to see.

Baird's beaked whales may slap the water's surface with their flippers or tails. This could be for communication, or just to play.

BAIRD'S BEAKED WHALE FACTS

Scientific Name: *Berardius bairdii*

Common Name: Baird's Beaked Whale

Other Names: Giant Bottlenose Whale, Northern Giant Bottlenose Whale, North Pacific Bottlenose Whale, Giant Four-Toothed Whale, North Pacific Four-Toothed Whale, Tsuchimbo, Tsuchi-kujira

Average Size:
Length - 39 to 42 feet (12 to 13 m)
Weight - 11 tons (10 t)

Where They Are Found: North Pacific Ocean and Bering Sea

When Baird's beaked whales surface, they rise straight up until their blowhole is exposed.

GLOSSARY

baleen - of or relating to the tough, hornlike material that hangs from the upper jaw of certain whales. Baleen is used to filter food.

blow - a mix of air and water droplets that are released when a marine mammal breathes.

blubber - a layer of fat in whales and other marine mammals. Blubber provides the whale with insulation, food storage, and padding.

Cetacea - an order of mammal, such as the whale, that lives in the water like fish. Members of this order are called cetaceans.

continental slope - the steep slope that drops from a continent to the ocean floor.

digest - to break down food into substances small enough for the body to absorb.

endangered - in danger of becoming extinct.

magnetic field - the space around a magnet or electric current in which the magnetic forces can be felt.

migrate - to move from one place to another, often to find food.

predator - an animal that kills and eats other animals.

pregnant - having one or more babies growing within the body.

spyhop - to raise the head above water to look around.

streamlined - having a shape that reduces the resistance to motion when moving through air or water.

temperate - having neither very hot nor very cold weather.

WEB SITES

To learn more about Baird's beaked whales, visit ABDO Publishing Company on the World Wide Web at **www.abdopub.com**. Web sites about these whales are featured on our Book Links page. These links are routinely monitored and updated to provide the most current information available.

INDEX